Let's Make Presents

Let's Make Presents

JACK CHALLONER, DAVE KING,
DAWN SIRETT, and ANGELA WILKES

DORLING KINDERSLEY
London • New York • Stuttgart • Moscow

How to use this book

Let's Make Presents is full of wonderful gifts to make for your family and friends from funny fridge magnets and photo frames to colourful painted bottles and papier-mâché brooches. Below are the points to look out for when using this book and a list of things to remember.

Equipment
Illustrated checklists show you which tools to have ready before you start each project.

The things you need
The items to collect for each project are clearly shown to help you check that you have everything you need.

Step-by-step
Step-by-step photographs and clear instructions tell you exactly what to do at each stage of a project.

Things to remember

- Read through all the instructions and gather together everything you will need before you begin a project.

- Put on an apron or an old shirt and roll up your sleeves before you start.

- Lay down lots of newspaper to protect your work surface and the floor.

- Be very careful when using scissors or sharp knives. Do not use them unless an adult is there to help you.

- When you need to take photographs for a project, hold your camera still when taking the pictures.

- Always open the windows when using oil-based varnish and ask an adult to clean the brush in white spirit for you.

- Put everything away when you have finished and clean up any mess.

A DORLING KINDERSLEY BOOK

Editor Fiona Campbell
Assistant Designer Caroline Potts
Managing Editor Jane Yorke
Managing Art Editor Chris Scollen
Production David Hyde
Photography Dave King
Illustrators Brian Delf and Coral Mula

First published in Great Britain in 1996
by Dorling Kindersley Limited,
9 Henrietta Street,
London WC2E 8PS

Copyright © 1996 Dorling Kindersley Limited, London
Projects originally published in *My First Activity Book*,
My First Batteries and Magnets Book, *My First Nature Book*,
My First Paint Book, and *My First Photography Book*
Copyright © 1989, 1992, 1990, 1994, 1994
Dorling Kindersley Limited, London

Visit us on the World Wide Web at http://www.dk.com

A CIP catalogue record for this book is available from the British Library.

ISBN 0-7513-5521-6

Colour reproduction by Colourscan
Printed and bound in Italy by L.E.G.O.

Contents

PHOTO FRAMES

Display your favourite photographs in fabulous stand up photo frames! Below are instructions for making a frame for a 15 cm x 10 cm (6 in. x 4 in.) standard size print. You can increase or reduce the size of this frame for larger or smaller prints. You can also make the format portrait or landscape by adapting the frame measurements to suit the format of your photograph.

EQUIPMENT

Scissors

Ruler   *Pencil*

Craft knife

You will need

Coloured card

Squares of coloured paper for decoration

Small beads for decoration

Patterned or textured paper for decoration

Strong glue

Making the frames

1 Cut out a rectangle of card 13 cm x 34 cm*. Measure halfway across the card and score along the middle mark.

2 Fold the card in half. Draw a rectangle in one half of the card with a 2 cm border all around it. Ask an adult to cut it out.

3 Glue a rectangle of card 16.5 cm x 12 cm inside the frame, over the hole. Glue along the short edges only, as shown.

6   * This will make a portrait frame big enough to frame a 15 cm x 10 cm (6 in. x 4 in.) print.

4 Cut out a thin strip of card about 18 cm long. Make a fold at one end. Glue the strip to the inside of the frame, as shown.

5 Ask an adult to make a slit in the other side of the frame. Slot the strip of card through the slit to make the frame stand up.

6 For decoration, glue on beads, textured paper, or paper cut-outs. When dry, slide a print into the side of the frame, as shown.

The finished frames

Here are some finished frames with photographs. Choose one of your favourite photographs to frame. You may need to trim the edges of the photograph so that it fits in the frame.

Colourful beads have been glued to this frame. You could also use dried beans, pasta, or shells.

A border of yellow card helps this photograph to stand out.

Try gluing patterned or textured paper to a frame. Cut the paper to fit the frame and angle the corners, as shown.

The cut-out paper shapes glued on to this frame make a pretty decoration.

7

BADGES AND BROOCHES

With some card, papier-mâché, and poster paint, you can design and paint a badge in any shape you like: try making your favourite animal, machine, vehicle, a round face, a sun, or a moon. The finished badges make wonderful gifts for your friends and family.

　　To make the papier-mâché mixture for the badges, you need to tear newspaper into tiny pieces and then mix the pieces with a little water and wallpaper paste. It should be a very smooth, dough-like mixture. Leave your papier-mâché badges to dry overnight before you start to paint them.

EQUIPMENT

Dish

Spoon

Pencil

Jar of water

Scissors

Saucer

You will need

Strong glue

Poster paints

Card

Thin paintbrush

Medium paintbrush

Brooch safety pins

21

A few sheets of newspaper

Thick wallpaper paste

Clear varnish

Making the badges

1 Draw a shape on card and cut it out. Tear newspaper into tiny pieces and mix it with a little water and wallpaper paste in an old dish.

2 Mash up the papier-mâché until it has the texture of dough. Put some on the card. Shape and leave to dry overnight.

3 Paint a design on the front and paint the back in one colour. Leave the badge to dry. Glue the pin to the back. Varnish the badge.

The finished badges

A thin paintbrush will help you to paint detail on the small badges. Here are some different designs.

The varnish makes the badges stronger and gives a shiny finish.

DINOSAUR

BOAT

Here papier-mâché has been shaped to look like fur.

DOG

SUN FACE

Papier mâché was built up to make the frame on this badge.

FRAMED PICTURE

Leave one colour to dry before you paint the next.

BUTTERFLY

CAR

PASTA JEWELLERY

Pasta is not just for eating! With a few handfuls of pasta shells, tubes and bows, some bright poster paints and multicoloured ribbons and beads, you can make your own exotic jewellery. Try making a necklace in colours to match your favourite jumper or skirt.

Shirring elastic

Rolled elastic

You will need

Pasta bows

Any pasta shapes with holes in the middle

Making beads

1 Paint some of the pasta shapes with thick poster paint. Paint tube-shaped pieces half at a time, letting them dry in between.

2 When the paint is completely dry, brush the pasta shapes with clear nail varnish. Varnish tubular shapes half at a time.

3 For a necklace using small pasta and beads, cut a piece of rolled elastic a little longer than you want the necklace to be.

Fine satin
ribbons

Clear nail varnish

Coloured nail varnish

Coloured wooden beads

Poster paints (including gold paint)

4 Thread pasta and beads on to the elastic. You may need to use a big needle. Tie the ends of the elastic in a knot.

5 Use shirring elastic to make necklaces from pasta bows. Thread the elastic through the tiny hole at the back of each bow.

6 Thread large, chunky pasta shapes or beads on to a piece of ribbon. Tie the ends in a bow to complete the necklace.

BOWS AND BEADS

Try making these necklaces or experiment with ideas of your own. Mix different types of pasta with contrasting beads and add brightly coloured ribbon bows.

JAZZY BRACELET

Paint ribbed macaroni with dark pink nail varnish. Thread on to elastic with green and yellow wooden beads.

RIBBONS AND BOWS

Use plain macaroni, blue pasta bows, small red beads, and pink ribbon. Thread the macaroni and beads on to elastic and tie it. Then tie small pieces of ribbon round the pasta bows and tie them to the elastic between the macaroni.

BOBBLE BEADS

For this necklace, use small pasta spirals and red, blue, and green wooden beads. You could make a matching bracelet, using a shorter piece of elastic.

GOLD CHOKER

Paint pasta bows gold and thread them on to shirring elastic so that they overlap.

CHUNKY NECKLACE

Use large macaroni beads for this necklace. Thread the pasta on to red ribbon and tie pieces of white ribbon between each bead.

13

PAINTED BOTTLES

Try turning empty bottles or jars into pretty vases and pots. Clean and dry the bottles or jars before you paint them. You can paint glass or plastic, but be very careful with glass: keep the bottle or jar on a table while you paint it. Finish with a coat of varnish so that the paint doesn't rub off.

EQUIPMENT

Jar of water *Saucer*

You will need

Medium paintbrush

Thin paintbrush

Poster paints

Empty bottles or jars (plastic or glass)

Clear varnish

PVA glue

Painting the bottle

1 Make sure the bottle or jar is clean and dry. Mix a little PVA glue with the paint. This helps the paint stick to the glass or plastic.

2 Paint a design on the bottle or jar. A simple idea is to dab dots of paint all over the bottle. Try using lots of different colours.

3 When the paint is dry, paint clear varnish on the bottle or jar. This will protect the paint and give a shiny finish.

14

The finished bottles and jars

The finished jars and bottles make perfect vases, pencil pots, or brush pots, and are excellent gifts for friends and family.

A border around the rim adds the finishing touch.

Here, one colour has been painted on to another.

PAINTING TIPS

- Keep the paint fairly thick so that it doesn't run.
- If you make a mistake, wipe the paint off before it dries and start again.

You can cover the container completely, or leave some glass or plastic showing.

A single pattern of zigzags, dots, and circles suits this narrow jar.

FRIDGE MAGNETS

Brighten up your kitchen with colourful decorations that cling to the fridge! Fridge magnets can come in all shapes and sizes and they are very easy to make. The magnets stick to the outside of the fridge, because it is made of steel. Try sticking them to other metal things around your home.

You will need

Glue

Coloured oven-hardening clay*

Plain self-hardening clay

Clear nail varnish

Poster paints

Small, flat magnets

What to do

1 Model any shape you like out of clay. Harden your shapes by following the instructions on the clay packet very carefully.

2 Paint the shapes made of plain clay and leave them to dry. Brush all of your shapes with clear nail varnish.

3 When the varnish is dry, glue a magnet to the back of each shape. Once the glue has set, the fridge magnets are ready to use.

* Ask an adult to help you to harden shapes made from this clay.

Magnetic fridge friends

The whale and the monster were made from coloured oven-hardening clays and the acrobats, fish, and dinosaur from plain, self-hardening clay, which was painted.

MAGNETIC
MINNOWS

WALLY

MONSTER
ATTRACTION

ACROBATIC
ADVENTURE

Arrange your acrobats in incredible balancing positions.

**DINOSAUR
ON DUTY**

Make an army of your favourite dinosaurs to guard the fridge.

CONCERTINA CARD

When you write to friends or relatives, why not send some photographs, too, showing the things you have done. Here, you can find out how to make a special photographic card to write a letter on.

You will need

Card for flap

Writing paper

Ribbon

Card for the concertina section

Hole punch

Glue stick

3 prints
(standard size:
15 cm x 10 cm;
6 in. x 4 in.)

Making the card

1 Cut out a 52.5 cm x 15 cm rectangle of card. Fold the card into five sections, each measuring 10.5 cm* as shown.

2 Glue 10.5 cm x 15 cm sheets of writing paper to four sections of the card. Glue an 8 cm x 15 cm strip of card to one end.

3 Fold over the strip of card to make a flap and angle the corners. Glue three prints to the other side of the card, as shown.

This will make a concertina card for three 15 cm x 10 cm (6 in. x 4 in.) prints.

The finished concertina card

When you have written your letter on the writing paper, punch a hole in the flap at the end of the concertina card. Thread a ribbon through the hole and round the folded card. Finally, tie the ribbon in a bow to hold the card together.

POST IT

If you are posting your card, put it into an envelope, write the address, and add a stamp.

Photographs

When tied, the ribbon holds the folded card together.

Hole made by a hole punch

Write the name of the person you are sending the card to on the front.

AN EXTRA SET

If you want to keep a set of the photographs you are using, take the negatives to a film processor (a shop that develops film) and get reprints made.

Flap with angled corners

A PHOTOGRAPHIC DISPLAY

Your friend can hang the card on a wall or stand it up on a shelf or mantelpiece.

Ribbon

CONCERTINA FOLDS

The concertina card is folded like a concertina (a type of musical instrument).

You can make a longer card with more photographs by adding more sections. You can also adjust the size of the card for larger or smaller prints.

19

WONDERFUL WAX

Wax and paint do not mix, but they can be used together to create an exciting picture. Here, thick paint is painted over wax crayon and then scratched off to make a picture of colourful fireworks. You can scratch out a night-time scene, an animal, a pattern, or anything you like.

You will need

Black poster paint

Light-coloured paper

Ice-lolly stick

Plastic knife

Thin paintbrush

Thick paintbrush

Wax crayons

Making the picture

1 Use brightly coloured wax crayons to draw a pattern on a sheet of paper. Fill the sheet of paper with the pattern.

2 Paint over the pattern with thick black paint. Make sure the pattern is completely covered. You may need two coats of paint.

3 When the paint is dry, draw a picture by scratching off the paint with a plastic knife, a lolly stick, or the end of a paintbrush.

The finished picture

When the black paint is scratched off, you can see the crayon underneath. Bright colours show up well, so use as many brightly coloured crayons as you have to make the pattern.

You can use the ice-lolly stick to scrape off large areas of paint.

The end of a paintbrush makes a medium mark.

The marks on the frame were made by scratching shapes into wet paint.

Painted card frame

Zigzags, swirls, and stars make brilliant, exploding fireworks!

FRAME IT!

A frame adds the finishing touch to a picture.

Thin or thick marks can be scratched out with the plastic knife.

21

PLANT PRESS

Pressing is a simple but magical way of preserving beautiful flowers and leaves so that they last for ever. Flowers with flat faces, like pansies, primroses and daisies are all easy to press. Pick dry, undamaged flowers and leaves and press them as quickly as you can, so that they keep their colour well*. Here you can find out how to make a simple plant press.

You will need

Flowers and leaves to press

Forget-me-nots

Daisies

EQUIPMENT

Scissors

Heavy books

* Never pick rare flowers.

Violas

Ivy leaves

Polyanthus

Primrose

What to do

Lots of white blotting paper

Some heavy books

1 Open the book. Cut out a piece of blotting paper about the same size as the open book. Fold the paper in half, then open it out.

2 Lay the blotting paper across the book. Arrange the plants flat, with space between them, on the right half of the paper.

3 Carefully fold the left side of the blotting paper over the plants. Then close the book over the blotting paper*.

To press more plants, do the same thing further on in the book.

4 Put some heavy books or magazines on top of the book, to weigh it down. Leave the plants to dry for at least four weeks.

23

Everlasting Flowers

After four weeks, your pressed plants should be dry and flat. You can glue them into your nature diary, to keep a record of what you have found, or make pictures with them. Start by making simple pictures with just one or two flowers, then experiment once you have had more practice. Here are some ideas for what you can make with your pressed flowers.

You will need

Thick paper or card

Rubber-based glue

Cotton buds

Pressed flowers and leaves

EQUIPMENT

Ruler

Scissors

Pencil

Making pictures

1 Measure and draw out the size you want your picture to be on the paper or card. Cut the paper out carefully.

2 Arrange where to put each flower and leaf. Pick up a flower and dab a tiny spot of glue on the back of it.

3 Gently position the flower where you want it. Do the same with the other flowers and leaves, then leave the glue to dry.

FLOWERY IDEAS

*You can make your own unique cards,
gift tags or bookmarks using simple
arrangements of pressed flowers or leaves.*

BOOKMARK

PICTURE

GIFT TAGS

MIX AND MATCH

You don't have to use just one photograph to make a picture. Why not take several photographs and join them together to make a panorama or montage? A panorama is a series of photographs of the same view, which are matched up to make one long picture. A montage is a mixture of different photographs that are stuck together. Here squares are cut out of old photographs, showing people, colours, and textures.

You will need

Old prints for montage

Croppers*

White paper

Masking tape

Glue stick

Thick coloured card

Prints for panorama

Taking a panorama

1 Choose a view to photograph and decide where you want your panorama to start and finish. Stand where you can see the whole view and do not move from this spot while taking the panorama. Turn your body from the waist so that you can see the start of the view in your viewfinder. Take the first picture.

2 Note where the first picture finishes. Turn your body from the waist, keeping your camera straight and part of your first picture still in the viewfinder (this will make your prints overlap so that you can join them together easily). Now take the next picture.

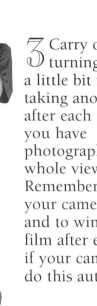

3 Carry on like this, turning your body a little bit more and taking another picture after each turn, until you have photographed the whole view. Remember to hold your camera firmly and to wind on your film after every shot, if your camera doesn't do this automatically.

Making a panorama

1 Lay down the first two prints and match them up. Tape them together with masking tape. Do this with all of the prints.

2 When you have done this, turn over the panorama and tape the prints on the back. Remove the tape on the front.

3 Rule lines along the top and bottom of the panorama to give a neat finish. Carefully cut along these lines with scissors.

Making a montage

4 Glue the prints on to white or coloured paper to create a narrow border. Then glue the panorama on to card, as shown.

1 Use your croppers to find interesting parts of old prints. Draw 3 cm squares around the prints and cut them out.

2 Arrange the squares and glue them on to a sheet of white paper. Then glue the sheet of paper on to some coloured card.

'Croppers' are two pieces of L-shaped card which become a frame, you can make bigger and smaller.

27

THE FINISHED PICTURES

The finished panorama and montage will make impressive pictures for your bedroom wall. You could make a montage of the people in your family to give your parents as a present. Look through your old photographs for the montage pictures. You could also look for images in magazines.

MONTAGE MIXTURES

Photographs of friends, animals, textures, colours, or a mixture of all of these, create a colourful montage.

PANORAMIC PICTURE

Match up your prints carefully, so they look like one long picture.

Take as many photographs as you need to complete the view.

Coloured card creates a frame.

A border of white paper helps the montage to stand out.

Here, photographs of such things as paper clips, plants, pebbles, and lentils, make a montage of contrasting textures.

28

You don't have to
use 3 cm squares.
You can make the
squares bigger or
smaller to suit
your montage.

Different faces, some
smiling, some eating,
some laughing, make
a fun montage.

USING
OLD PRINTS

A montage is a clever
way of using old
photographs that are not
good enough to frame or
put in an album,
but are too
interesting to
throw away.

MATCHING UP

Don't worry if your
panorama doesn't
match up exactly.
It will still look like
one picture.

Portrait or landscape photographs
can be used in a panorama. Here,
portrait photographs were used.

29

GIFT BAGS

Here, you can find out how to make printing blocks out of modelling clay and create fabulous patterned paper. Use thick paint, sponges, and an old baking tray. You can turn your printed paper into gift bags, or simply use the sheets as wrapping paper. The gift bags are also useful for storing things in.

EQUIPMENT

Pencil

Scissors

Hole punch

Baking tray and household sponges

Ruler

Jar of water

You will need

Gift ribbon

Modelling clay

Paintbrush

Thick paper

Plastic knife

Poster paints

PVA glue

Tracing paper

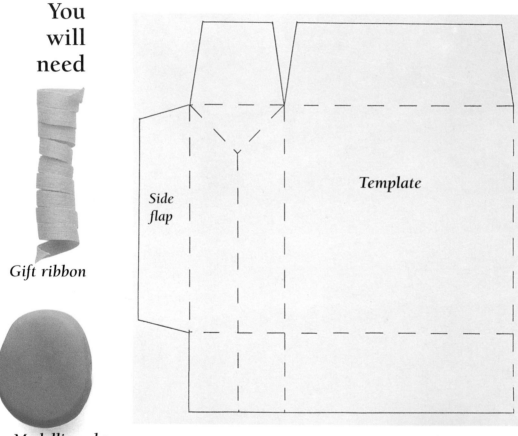

Side flap

Template

Making the gift bag

1 Shape a lump of modelling clay. Flatten one side and make marks in it. Use different shaped lumps to make different prints.*

2 Press the clay into the printing pad. Then print a pattern on a sheet of paper. Leave the paint to dry before printing a new colour.

3 Trace the template onto tracing paper with a pencil. Then colour over the lines with the pencil, as shown.

Here, dots are made in a roll of clay and crossed lines are made in a round lump.

4 Turn over the tracing paper. Place it on the back of the dry printed sheet of paper. Draw over the template twice, as shown.**

5 Cut out the bag pattern. Score along all the lines and fold them, as shown, to make the bag. Glue the side flap and let it dry.

6 Glue the bottom flaps. You can put something heavy in the bag to help them to stick. When dry, punch two holes in the top.

The finished gift bags

Here are some ideas for patterns and colours to print. You can make different sized bags by changing the size of the template.

The printing block for the circles was made by pressing a button into a round lump of clay.

A diamond was marked into a square of clay to make the printing block for the blue diamonds.

For this block, the outline of a boat was marked into clay and then the whole boat was cut out.

For the waves block, the outline of waves was marked into clay and then the clay around the outline was cut away.

GIFT TAGS

Cut out small rectangles of the paper and fold them to make tags. You can then cut the folded rectangles into other shapes, if you wish. Use a hole punch to make a hole for the ribbon.

Circles and diamonds

Flowers

**Leave off the side flap the second time you draw over the lines of the template.

31